MW00948374

Prescription Scriptures

Vol. 3 Marriage

(What God Has Joined Together)

Photographed by: Sunni Barbosa-Reeves and Tommy Reeves

Prescription Scriptures

Vol. 3 Marriage

(What God Has Joined Together)

ISBN-ISBN-13:

978-1721087129

ISBN-10:
1721087125

Copyright © 2018 by Sunni Barbosa- Reeves & Tommy Reeves

Published by GODLYGirl Entertainment.

789 Hammond Dr. Suite # 2701

Sandy Springs GA, 30328

Search Sunni Barbosa on Amazon.com

Thank You for Supporting Positive Media!

These teachings have been inspired by:

Pastor Monique

&

Walter Rice
(World Outreach Christian Center)

**May God Himself continue to reward your obedience!
Thank you**

This book is dedicated to my Amazing Husband and Better Half,

Tommy Benard Reeves

You are the dearest, most loving man I have ever known and now you are the only man I want to know! I have truly been blessed with a man after GODs own heart. You were brave and giving enough to take on an awesome responsibility, that many could not have handled, even if they wanted too. You are indeed one of GODs special creatures and you are being and will continue to be rewarded for your wonderful works great and small. to you I will always be in a constant state of appreciation!

THANK YOU

Love, Sunni

This is a book that allows you to save time, in a time of need by taking you straight to the marriage scriptures of the Bible without the search. Nothing is too big for God.

All you gotta do is believe.

This is what you will need to do:

Speak it into Existence! These Scriptures are to be recited as many times as needed, the more the better. (There are no words more powerful then Gods Words, use them to stab and poke holes in the devil's butt! Now, Doesn't that sound like FUN?)

1. Make GOD the head of your marriage and keep him there, pleasing your spouse is not enough, as long as GOD is pleased with you, your spouse will be too! Always remembering that if you hurt your spouse, you hurt GOD and the gift that HE has blessed you with.
2. Believe! (True Faith) Believing that God is able and will protect you according to His own words.

3. Be Proactive! Don't wait for things to go wrong in your marriage, take the necessary steps to ensure that certain things don't go wrong whenever possible.

4. Communicate! Communicate! Communicate! When you are open and honest with each other this leaves little to no space for the enemy to enter.

5. Last but definitely not least, the more LOVE you make the better off you both will be! That's right; sex it on up! Hang from the rafters if you have too, whatever you do remain Faithful and have Fun!

Genesis 2:22

"And the rib, which the LORD God had taken from man, made he a woman, and brought her unto the man. And Adam said, this is now bone of my bones, and flesh of my flesh: she shall be called Woman, because she was taken out of Man.

Proverb 20:7

The righteous man walk in his integrity;
His children are blessed after him.

Proverbs 18:22

**He who finds a wife finds a good thing
and obtains favor from the LORD.**

Proverbs 12:4

"An excellent wife is the crown of her husband, but she who causes shame is like rottenness in his bones."

Proverbs 11:22

As a ring of gold in as a swine's snout, so is a lovely woman who lacks discretion.

Proverbs 14:1

The wise woman builds her house, But the foolish pulls it down with her hands.

Proverbs 19:14

House and riches are inheritance of fathers: and a prudent wife is from the LORD.

Proverbs 20:6

Most men will proclaim each his own goodness, but who can find a faithful man?

Proverb 31:10

A wife of noble character who can find?
She is worth far more than rubies.

Proverbs 21:9

It is better to live in a corner of the housetop than in a house shared with a quarrelsome wife.

Proverbs 5:19

As a loving deer and graceful doe, Let her breasts satisfy you at all times; And always be enraptured with her love.

Genesis 2: 24

Therefore a man shall leave his father and his mother and be joined to his wife, and they shall become one flesh.

Deuteronomy 24:5

When a man hath taken a new wife, he shall not go out to war, or be charged with any business; he shall be free at home one year and bring happiness to his wife whom he has taken.

1 Corinthians 7:2

Nevertheless, because of sexual immorality, let each man have his own wife, and let each woman have her own husband.

1 Corinthians 7:3

Let the husband render to his wife the affection due her, and likewise also the wife to her husband.

Ephesians 5:28

So husbands ought to love their own wives as their own bodies; he who loves his wife loves himself.

Ephesians 5:29

For no one ever hated his own flesh, but nourishes and cherishes it, just as the LORD does the church.

Matthew 19:6

So then, they are no longer two, but one flesh. Therefore, what God has joined together, let no one separate."

1 Corinthians 7:14

For the unbelieving husband has been sanctified through his wife, and the unbelieving wife has been sanctified through her believing husband. Otherwise your children would be unclean, but as it is, they are holy.

1 Corinthians 7:15

*But if the unbeliever leaves, let it be so.
The brother or the sister is not under
bondage in such cases.*

LEVITICUS 18:22

Thou shalt not lie with mankind, as with womankind; it is abomination.

Hebrews 13: 4

Marriage is honorable among all, and the bed undefiled; but fornicators and adulterers GOD will judge.

Corinthians 7:4

The wife does not have authority over her own body, but the husband does. And likewise, the husband does not have authority over his own body, but the wife does.

My Gift to You.

I offer you, my utmost transparency and sincere vulnerability when I tell you that, I kissed a lot of frogs before kissing my King and True Soul Mate. I'm sure I could have saved myself a lot of trouble by simply waiting. Unfortunately, today waiting is just not something a lot of us are prepared to do for much of anything anymore. However, in my life experience, I must tell you that GOD HIMSELF; did not allow my true soul mate to come to me until I was fully, completely and wholly aware that GOD that was, is and always will be 1st in my life, GOD is my EVERYTHING!!!

HE is:

My Mother

My Father

My Husband

My Doctor

My Police

My Provider

My Ultimate Sustainer

Thank you, GOD, without you I am nothing.

Made in the USA
Columbia, SC
19 April 2021